A Weed is a Flower:

The Life of
George Washington Carver

written and illustrated by *Aliki*

Prentice-Hall, Inc., Englewood Cliffs, N.J.

Seventh Printing......... March, 1972

©1965 by Aliki Brandenberg

Library of Congress Catalog Card Number: 65-25223

Printed in the United States of America

J-94786

for Lisa, Jim and Stephen

When George Washington Carver was born, he had many things against him. He was a sick, weak, little baby. His father had just died, and his mother was left alone to care for him and for his brother, James. And even worse, he was the son of slaves. There was no hope for the future.

But George Washington Carver was no ordinary man. He was a man who turned evil into good, despair into hope and hatred into love. He was a man who devoted his whole life to helping his people and the world around him.

This is his story.

George Washington Carver was born in Missouri in 1860—more than a hundred years ago. It was a terrible time. Mean men rode silently in the night, kidnapping slaves from their owners and harming those who tried to stop them.

One night, a band of these men rode up to the farm of Moses Carver, who owned George and his mother, Mary. Everyone ran in fear. But before Mary could hide her baby, the men came and snatched them both, and rode away into the night.

Moses Carver sent a man to look for them.
Mary was never found. But in a few days,
the man returned with a small bundle wrapped
in his coat and tied to the back of his saddle.
It was the baby, George.

Moses and his wife, Susan, cared for Mary's children. George remained small and weak. But as he grew, they saw he was an unusual child. He wanted to know about everything around him. He asked about the rain, the flowers, and the insects. He asked questions the Carvers couldn't answer.

When he was very young, George kept a garden where he spent hours each day caring for his plants. If they weren't growing well, he found out why. Soon they were healthy and blooming. In winter he covered his plants to protect them. In spring he planted new seeds. George looked after each plant as though it was the only one in his garden.

Neighbors began to ask George's advice about their plants, and soon he was known as the Plant Doctor.

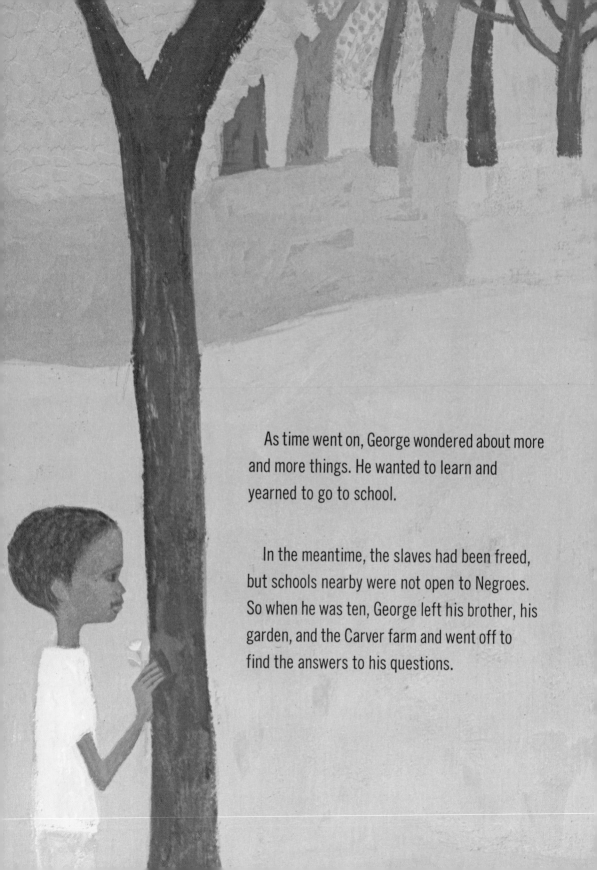

As time went on, George wondered about more
and more things. He wanted to learn and
yearned to go to school.

In the meantime, the slaves had been freed,
but schools nearby were not open to Negroes.
So when he was ten, George left his brother, his
garden, and the Carver farm and went off to
find the answers to his questions.

Wherever George Washington Carver found schools, he stayed. He worked for people to earn his keep. He scrubbed their floors, washed their clothes, and baked their bread. Whatever George did, he did well. Even the smallest chore was important to him.

Some people took George in as their son. First he stayed with Mariah and Andy Watkins, who were like parents to him. Then he moved to Kansas and lived with "Aunt" Lucy and "Uncle" Seymour. They, too, loved this quiet boy who was so willing to help.

George worked hard for many years, always trying to save enough money for college. Other boys, who had parents to help them, were able to enter college much sooner than George. He was thirty before he had saved enough. Still, it was not that simple. All colleges would not admit Negroes, even if they had the money to pay.

George was not discouraged. He moved to Iowa, and found a college which was glad to have a Negro student.

At college, George continued to work. He opened a laundry where he washed his schoolmates' clothes.

And, he continued to learn. His teachers and friends soon realized that this earnest young man was bursting with talents. He played the piano, he sang beautifully, and he was an outstanding painter. In fact, for a time he thought of becoming an artist.

But the more George thought of what he wanted to do, the more he wanted to help his people, and he remembered that his neighbors used to call him the Plant Doctor.

He had never forgotten his love for plants. In all the years he had wandered, he always had something growing in his room.

So, George Washington Carver chose to study agriculture. He learned about plants, flowers, and soil. He learned the names of the weeds. Even they were important to him. He often said: a weed is a flower growing in the wrong place.

He still asked questions. If no person or book could answer them, he found the answers himself. He experimented with his own plants, and found secrets no one else knew.

When George finished college, he began to teach. He was asked to go to Alabama, where a college for Negroes needed his talent. It was there, at Tuskegee Institute, that George Washington Carver made his life.

In Alabama, Professor Carver taught his students and the poor Negro farmers, who earned their livelihood from the soil. He taught them how to make their crops grow better.

Most of the farmers raised cotton. But sometimes the crops were destroyed by rain or insects, and the farmers couldn't earn enough to eat.

Professor Carver told them to plant other things as well. Sweet potatoes and peanuts were good crops. They were easy to grow. He said that raising only cotton harmed the soil. It was better if different crops were planted each year.

The farmers did not want to listen. They were afraid to plant peanuts and sweet potatoes. They were sure that no one would buy them.

But Professor Carver had experimented in his laboratory. He had found that many things could be made from the sweet potato. He made soap, coffee, and starch. He made more than a hundred things from the sweet potato.

And even though people in those days called peanuts "monkey food," Professor Carver said they were good for people, too. Besides, he found that still more things could be made from the peanut. Paper, ink, shaving cream, sauces, linoleum, shampoo, and even milk! In fact, he made three hundred different products from the peanut.

Once, when important guests were expected at Tuskegee, Dr. Carver chose the menu. The guests sat around the table and enjoyed a meal of soup, creamed mock chicken, bread, salad, coffee, candy, cake, and ice cream. Imagine their surprise when they learned that the meal was made entirely from peanuts!

Slowly, the farmers listened to George Washington Carver. They planted peanuts and sweet potatoes, and before they knew it these became two of the most important crops in Alabama.

Soon the whole country knew about Dr. Carver and the great things he was doing. He was honored by Presidents and other important people. Every day, his mailbox bulged with letters from farmers and scientists who wanted his advice. He was offered great sums of money, which he turned down. Money was not important to him. He did not even bother to cash many of the checks he received.

Throughout his life, George Washington Carver asked nothing of others. He sought only to help. He lived alone and tended to his own needs. He washed his clothes and patched them, too. He used the soap he made and ate the food he grew.

Dr. Carver was asked to speak in many parts of the world, but he did not leave Tuskegee often. He had things to do. He continued to paint. He worked in his greenhouse and in his laboratory, where he discovered many things. He discovered that dyes could be made from plants, and colors from the Alabama clay. Even when he was over eighty and close to death, Dr. Carver kept working. Night after night, while the rest of the town lay asleep, a light still shone in his window.

The baby born with no hope for the future grew into one of the great scientists of his country. George Washington Carver, with his goodness and devotion, helped not only his own people, but all peoples of the world.